LIVELY LISTENING

GRADES 4-6

WRITTEN AND ILLUSTRATED BY BEVERLY ARMSTRONG

The Learning Works

LIVELY LISTENING

FEATURES OF LIVELY LISTENING

The exercises in Lively Listening are designed to involve children in grades 4-6 in active listening. Listening means not only hearing but paying attention to what is heard. The exercises in this book combine whimsical pictures with oral directions to help improve listening skills:

HOW TO USE LIVELY LISTENING

1. Each student needs a copy of the activity sheet, crayons, and a pencil.

2. Explain to the students that they are to listen *very* carefully as you read the directions because you will say each step only once. Instruct students to do only what you tell them.

3. Read each step in the directions slowly and clearly.

4. Pause long enough after each step to give students time to complete what they have been told to do, but don't allow the pace to drag. Do *not* repeat any direction.

The purchase of this book entitles the individual teacher to reproduce copies for use in the classroom.

The reproduction of any part for an entire school or school system or for commercial use is strictly prohibited.

No form of this work may be reproduced or transmitted or recorded without written permission from the publisher.

LARRY LARIAT LOOK-ALIKES

LES

LANCE

LOU

LEON

LUKE

LEE

LENNIE

LINK

KAREN'S KITTEN

PICK A WINNER

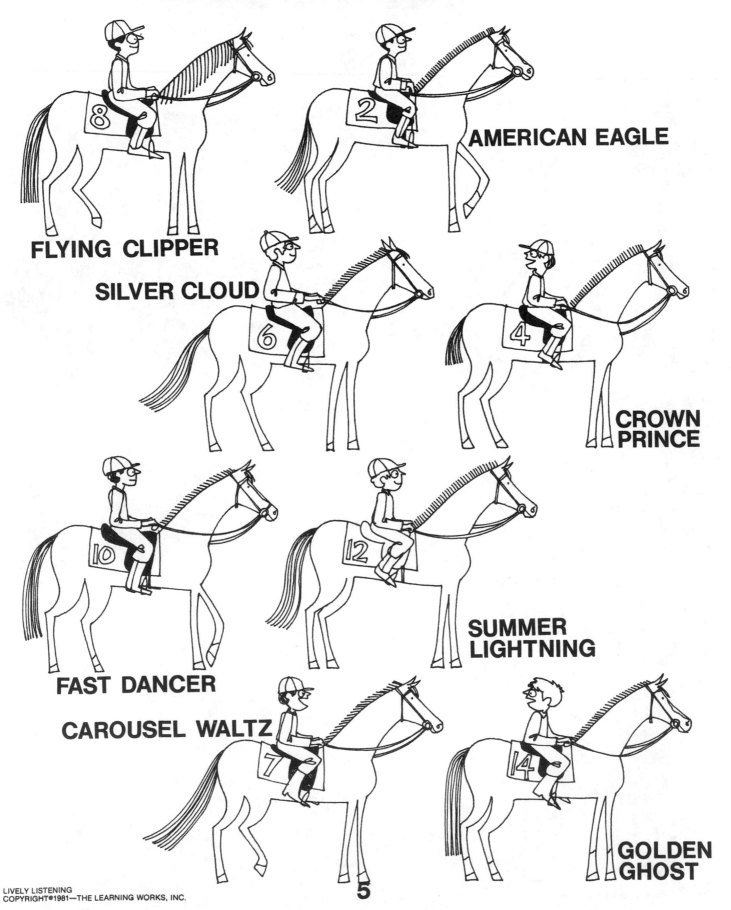

FLYING CLIPPER

AMERICAN EAGLE

SILVER CLOUD

CROWN PRINCE

FAST DANCER

SUMMER LIGHTNING

CAROUSEL WALTZ

GOLDEN GHOST

LIVELY LISTENING
COPYRIGHT©1981—THE LEARNING WORKS, INC.

TOP DOG

AIREDALE

NEWFOUNDLAND

PUG

BASSET

BEAGLE

BASENJI

DACHSHUND

POODLE

FIND THE SPY

STAN

SULLY

SKIP

SIGMUND

SHERMAN

SID

SYLVESTER

STEVE

SKATING FIGURES

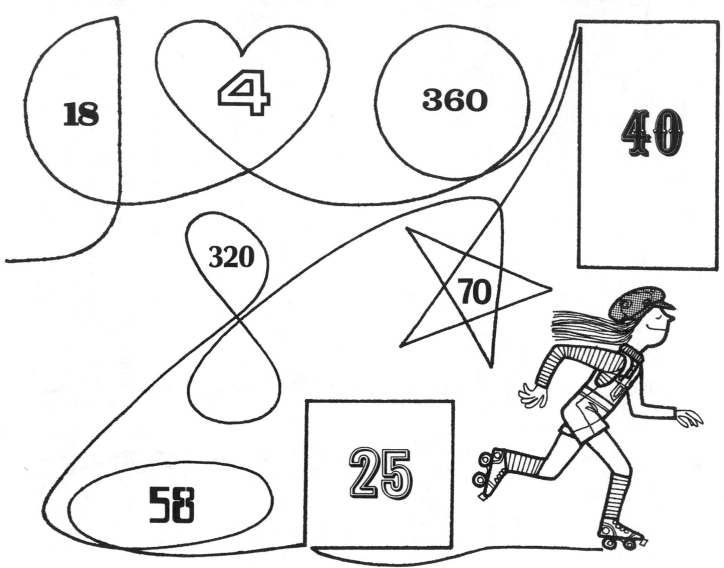

SKATING FIGURES

1. More than _____ million people in the United States have skated at least once.
2. Roller skating was invented in Holland in the _____th century.
3. In 1927, Arthur Allegretti skated 500 miles from Buffalo to New York City in only _____ hours.
4. You can burn up to _____ calories per hour by roller skating.
5. The speed record for roller skating is more than _____ miles per hour.
6. A woman skated across the United States _____ years before any man did.
7. There are more than _____ thousand roller skating rinks in the United States.
8. A roller skating marathon record of more than _____ hours was set in 1977.

ALPHABET SOUP

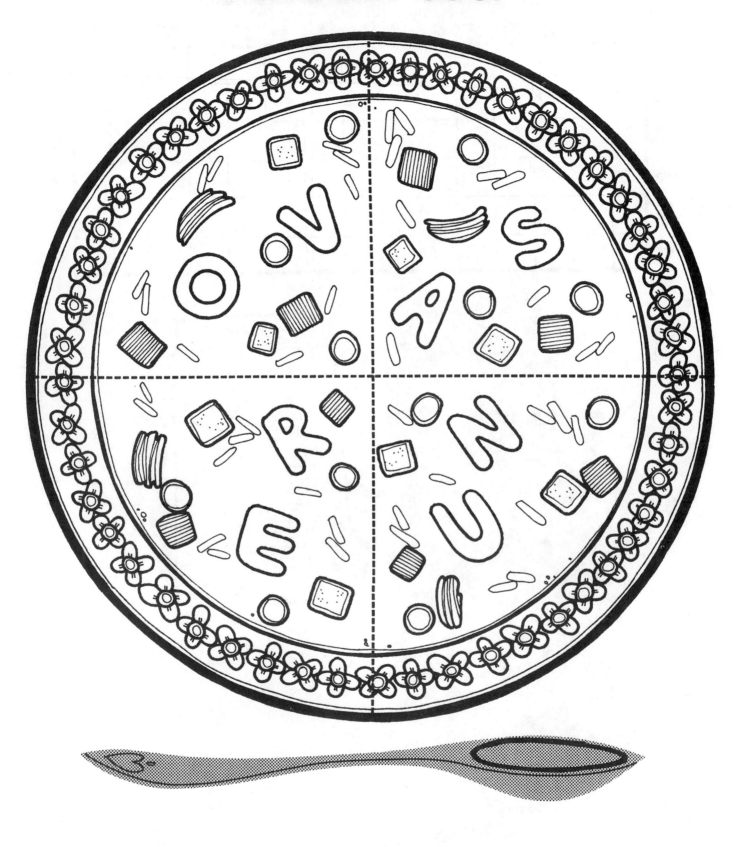

POTATO PUZZLE

	A	B	C	D	E	F	G	H	I	J	K	L	M	N	O	
1																1
2																2
3																3
4																4
5																5
6																6

FIX THE X-RAY

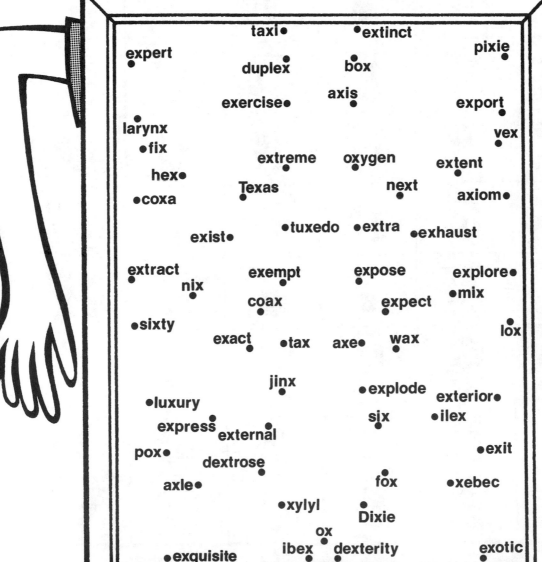

taxi • extinct

expert •

pixie

duplex • box

axis

exercise • export

larynx vex

• fix

extreme oxygen extent

hex • next

• coxa Texas axiom •

• tuxedo • extra • exhaust

exist •

extract • explore •

nix expose • mix

exempt

coax expect

• sixty lox

exact • tax axe • wax

jinx

• explode exterior •

• luxury six • ilex

express external

pox • • exit

dextrose

axle • fox • xebec

• xylyl

Dixie

ox

• exquisite ibex dexterity exotic

1,840 WHATS?

	1	2	3	4	5	6
A	C	M	V	T	H	S
B	M	G	I	N	D	W
C	F	X	A	E	N	U
D	E	S	F	O	Y	J
E	Z	B	G	R	V	M
F	H	Q	O	A	D	W
G	D	X	I	E	B	R
H	O	S	K	Y	J	C
I	B	R	T	A	P	K
J	L	Z	Q	U	B	M

NOISY GHOST

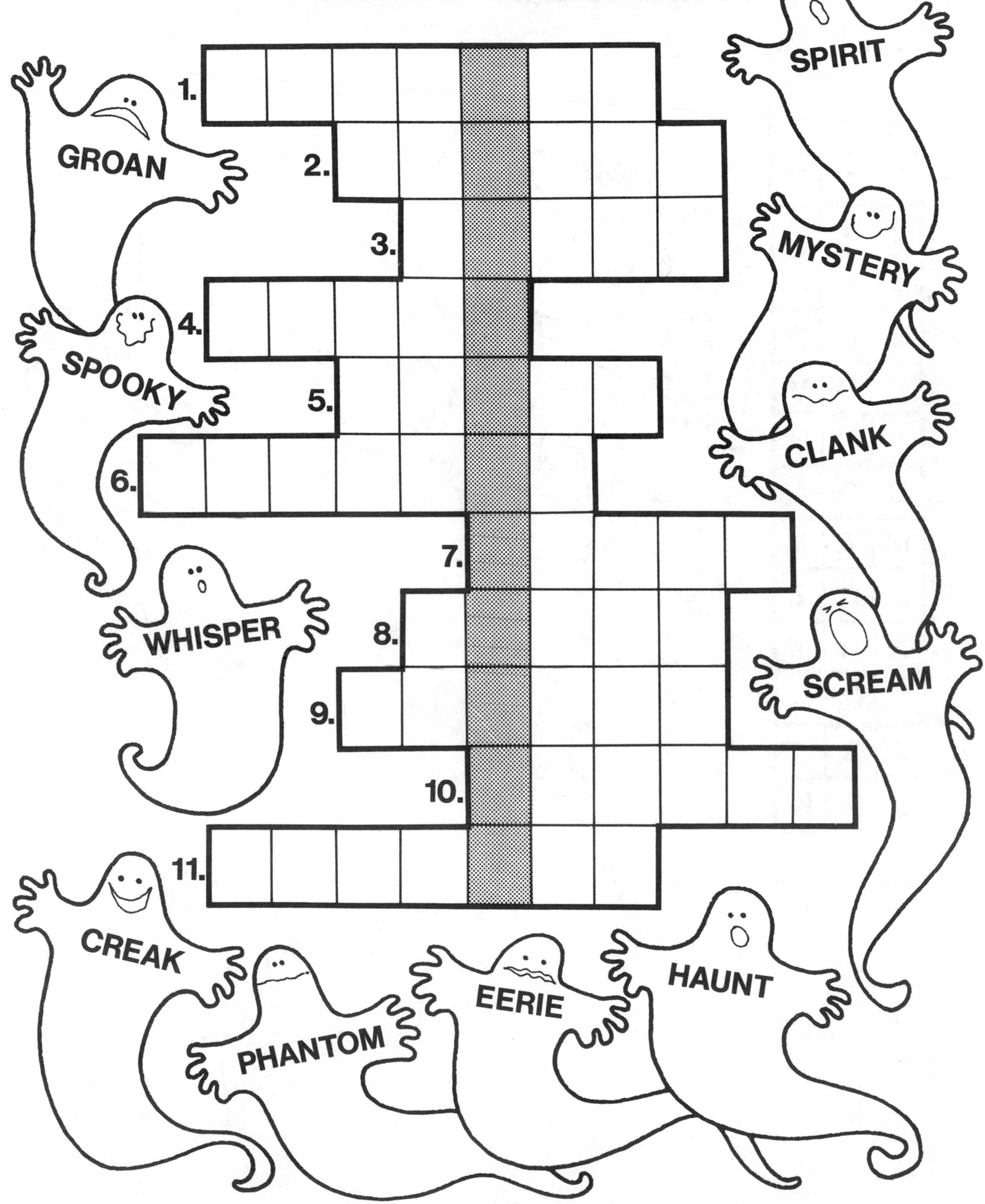

SPIRIT

GROAN

MYSTERY

1.

2.

3.

4.

SPOOKY

5.

CLANK

6.

7.

WHISPER

8.

SCREAM

9.

10.

11.

CREAK

PHANTOM

EERIE

HAUNT

A SKY FULL OF KITES

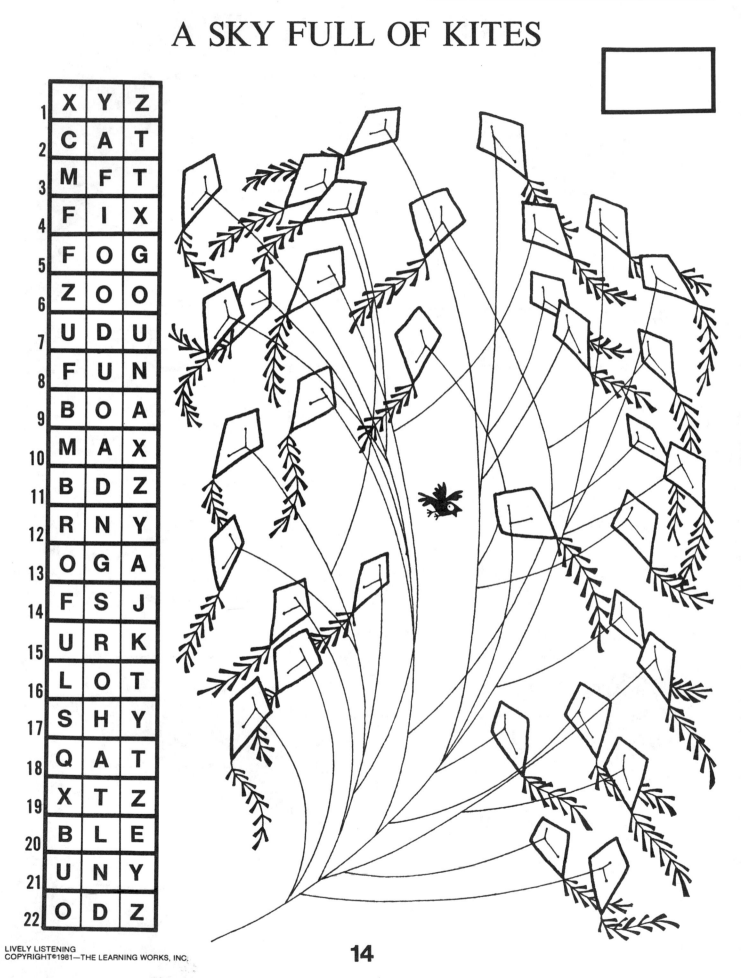

1	X	Y	Z
2	C	A	T
3	M	F	T
4	F	I	X
5	F	O	G
6	Z	O	O
7	U	D	U
8	F	U	N
9	B	O	A
10	M	A	X
11	B	D	Z
12	R	N	Y
13	O	G	A
14	F	S	J
15	U	R	K
16	L	O	T
17	S	H	Y
18	Q	A	T
19	X	T	Z
20	B	L	E
21	U	N	Y
22	O	D	Z

TRICKY TOY

1	2	3	4	5	6	7	8	9	10	11	12

FIND THE FOOD

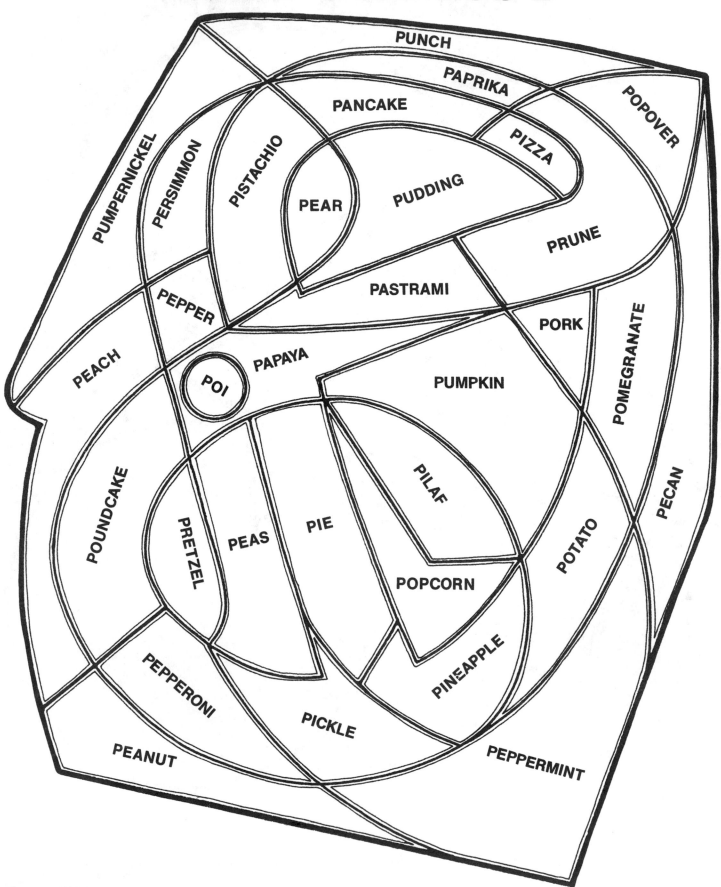

WHAT HAPPENED?

1	2	3	4	5	6	7	8	9	10

11	12	13	14	15	16	17	18	19	20	21

HIDDEN TONGUE TWISTER

18

FAMOUS FOODS

Name _____

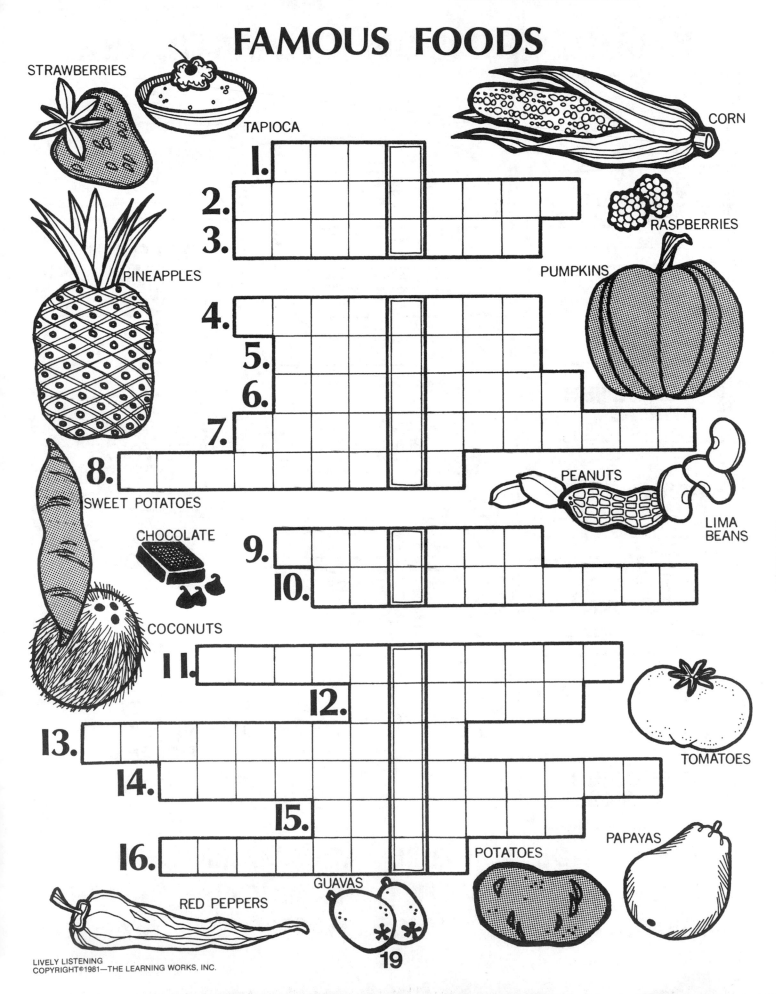

STRAWBERRIES

TAPIOCA

CORN

RASPBERRIES

PINEAPPLES

PUMPKINS

SWEET POTATOES

CHOCOLATE

PEANUTS

LIMA BEANS

COCONUTS

TOMATOES

RED PEPPERS

GUAVAS

POTATOES

PAPAYAS

1.
2.
3.
4.
5.
6.
7.
8.
9.
10.
11.
12.
13.
14.
15.
16.

19

KHAKI, CRIMSON, CHARTREUSE

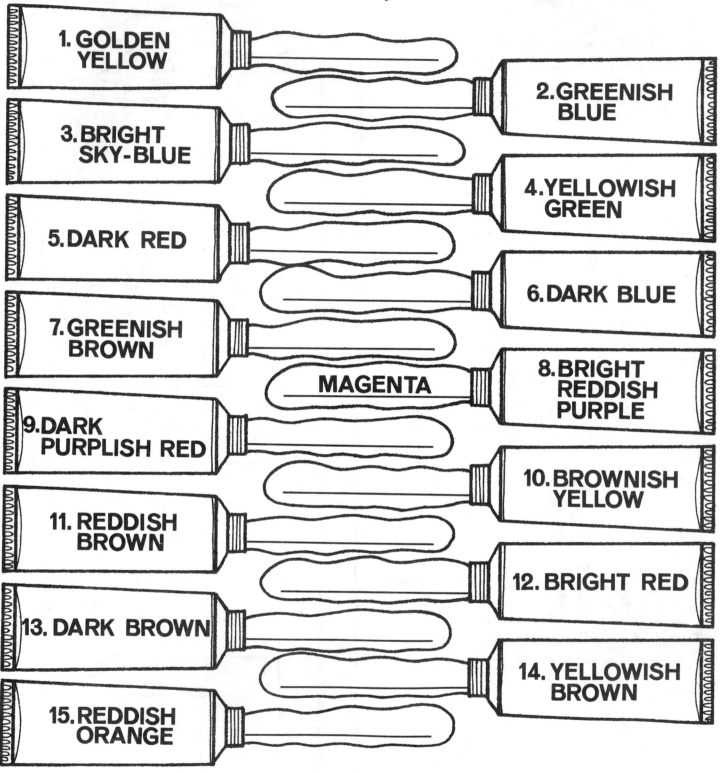

1. GOLDEN YELLOW

2. GREENISH BLUE

3. BRIGHT SKY-BLUE

4. YELLOWISH GREEN

5. DARK RED

6. DARK BLUE

7. GREENISH BROWN

MAGENTA

8. BRIGHT REDDISH PURPLE

9. DARK PURPLISH RED

10. BROWNISH YELLOW

11. REDDISH BROWN

12. BRIGHT RED

13. DARK BROWN

14. YELLOWISH BROWN

15. REDDISH ORANGE

RUSSET   INDIGO   AZURE   AQUAMARINE   CRIMSON

AMBER   SEPIA   OCHER   VERMILION   SCARLET

MAGENTA   UMBER   KHAKI   CHARTREUSE   MAROON

HIPPO RIDDLE

#		
1.	A	B
2.	E	X
3.	C	O
4.	M	A
5.	U	N
6.	I	S
7.	M	E
8.	A	M
9.	I	D
10.	U	T
11.	F	Z
12.	E	W
13.	A	L
14.	U	S
15.	M	O
16.	T	A
17.	N	I
18.	B	E
19.	D	U

#		
20.	T	E
21.	S	O
22.	I	F
23.	T	O
24.	U	H
25.	P	E
26.	R	X
27.	A	C
28.	H	I
29.	I	H
30.	O	C
31.	K	U
32.	Z	E
33.	O	N

WALK

Name _____

NAME THAT NOTE

SCREAM
THUD
SCREECH
CHIRP
SMACK
HISS
JINGLE
GROWL
GRIND
HUM
RATTLE
SQUEAK
SNAP
TWANG
VAROOM
SLURP
CRASH
TWEET

Name _____

FIND THE FACE

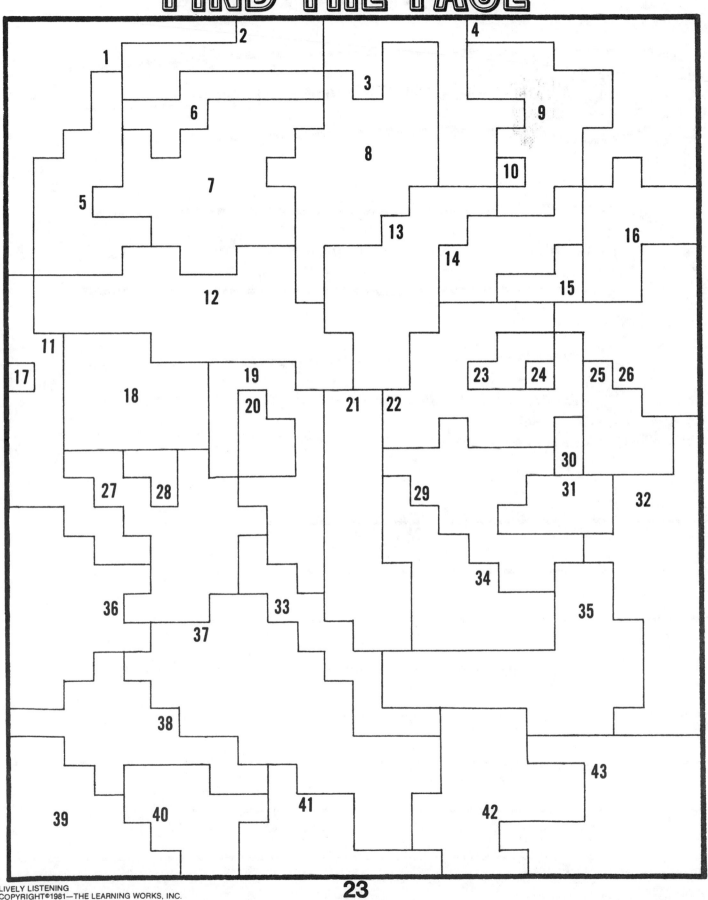

SNAKE FACTS

1. SNAKES 2. BIGGER 3. SWIMMERS 4. THEIR 5. TONGUES 6. SWALLOW

7. EYES 8. ARE 9. STING 10. TAILS 11. POISONOUS 12. DEAF 13. CLOSE 14. CAN'T 15. THINGS

16. WITH 17. NOT 18. HEADS 19. OR 20. THAN 21. GOOD 22. CAN 23. MOST

X _____   Q _____   N _____   V _____■

A _____   X _____   Q _____   S _____   P _____■

X _____   Z _____   G _____   D _____

        W _____   L _____   K _____   M _____■

X _____   Q _____   C _____■

X _____   Z _____   H _____   W _____   J _____■

X _____   U _____   R _____   O _____

        F _____   I _____   W _____   B _____■

Name _____

WHAT'S A MENAGERIE?

1. ☐
2. ☐
3. ☐
4. ☐
5. ☐
6. ☐
7. ☐
8. ☐
9. ☐
10. ☐
11. ☐
12. ☐
13. ☐
14. ☐
15. ☐
16. ☐
17. ☐
18. ☐
19. ☐
20. ☐

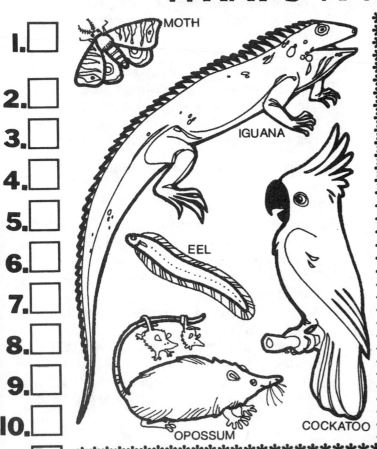
MOTH
IGUANA
EEL
OPOSSUM
COCKATOO

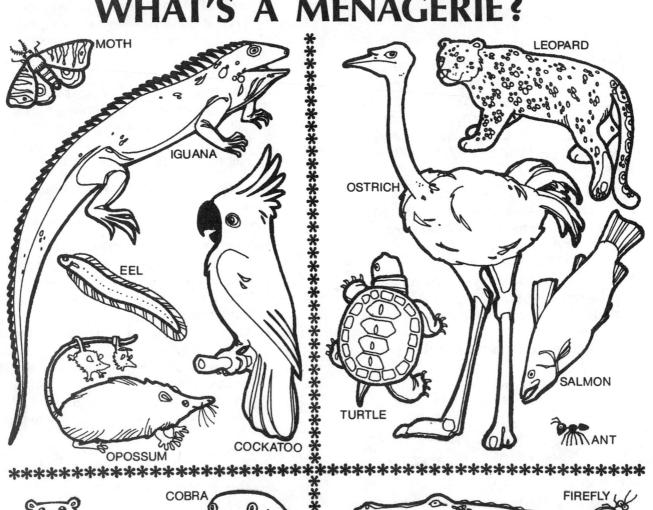
LEOPARD
OSTRICH
TURTLE
SALMON
ANT

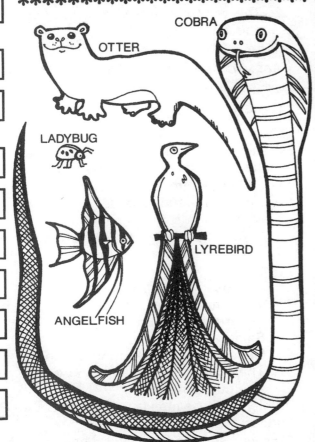
OTTER
COBRA
LADYBUG
ANGELFISH
LYREBIRD

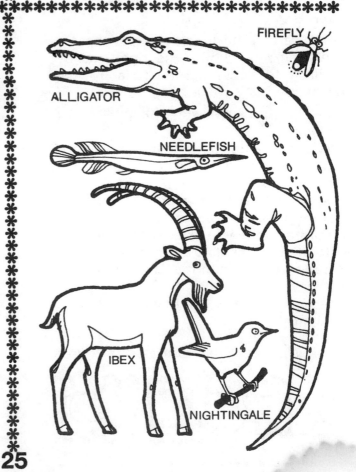
FIREFLY
ALLIGATOR
NEEDLEFISH
IBEX
NIGHTINGALE

ORAL DIRECTIONS and ANSWERS

LARRY LARIAT LOOK-ALIKES—page 3

Larry Lariat, the rodeo star, is having a contest to see who can look the most like him. These men have entered the contest, and one looks just like Larry! Listen carefully, and cross out the cowboys who don't look like Larry.

1. Larry always wears a **white hat.**
2. Of course he wears **cowboy boots**, too.
3. He says that his **checked shirt** brings good luck and helps him win prizes.
4. Over his shirt he wears a **vest.**
5. Although he is not a sheriff, he wears a **star-shaped badge.**
6. He thinks his **moustache** makes him look handsome.
7. He always carries a **lariat** to catch cows and do tricks with.

Answer: Who looks the most like Larry Lariat? **Luke.**

KAREN'S KITTEN—page 4

Karen's parents have said she can have a kitten! Help her choose the right one by crossing out the ones that aren't exactly what she wants.

1. Karen wants a kitten with a **happy smile** on its face.
2. She wants a kitten that has **stripes or spots.**
3. Karen's father would like her to get a kitten that **mews quietly.**
4. She would like a kitten with **curly whiskers.**
5. Karen's mother is worried about the furniture and would like her to choose a kitten that keeps its **claws tucked in.**
6. Karen wants a kitten that is **wide awake,** not lazy.
7. She wants a kitten that holds its **tail up straight.**

Answer: The best kitten for Karen is **Pogo.**

PICK A WINNER—page 5

Which of these horses will win the race? Cross out each horse that is **not** the winner.

1. The winning horse has a long tail.
2. His ears are pointed forward with excitement.
3. His jockey is wearing his lucky cap.
4. The horse that will win has a short mane.
5. He is wearing a dark-colored saddle.
6. The winner has an even number on his blanket.
7. His name does not begin with vowels.

Answer: The winner is **Fast Dancer.**

TOP DOG—page 6

Follow the directions to find out which breed of dog is the winner at this dog show. Cross out the nonwinners.

1. The winning dog has more than three letters in its name.
2. Its name does not start and end with the same letter.
3. The winner's name does not contain a double consonant.
4. The name does not contain the letter J.
5. The winner's name contains fewer than twelve letters.
6. The name does not contain a double vowel.
7. The winner's name does not begin and end with vowels.

Draw a circle around the winner.

Answer: The winning dog is the **beagle.**

FIND THE SPY—page 7

One of these men is really Sly Sam Sneakpeep, international spy. The information you are about to be given will help you identify him. Listen carefully, and cross out the other suspects as you find out that they are not Mr. Sneakpeep.

1. Sly Sam Sneakpeep always wears a hat.
2. Sam is standing with his hands in his pockets.
3. He does not wear glasses.
4. Sly Sam is carrying something under his left arm.
5. Sam has a long nose.
6. He is wearing dark-colored shoes.
7. The collar of Sam's coat is turned up around his neck.

Which of these men is really Sam? Write **Spy** under him.

Answer: **Sigmund** *is really Sam.*

SKATING FIGURES—page 8

Use the numbers in the shapes to fill in the skating facts.

1. Fill in the first fact with the number inside the star.
2. Fill in the seventh fact with the number inside the heart.
3. Fill in the fourth fact with the number inside the circle.
4. Fill in the second fact with the number inside the half circle.
5. Fill in the eighth fact with the number inside the figure eight.
6. Fill in the fifth fact with the number inside the oval.
7. Fill in the third fact with the number inside the square.
8. Fill in the sixth fact with the number inside the rectangle.

ALPHABET SOUP—page 9

Follow the directions to spell a word that means **very hungry**.

1. On the second line, write the vowel that is in the upper right part of the bowl.
2. On the seventh line, write the vowel that is in the lower right part of the bowl.
3. On the third line, write the consonant that is in the upper left part of the bowl.
4. On the fifth line, write the consonant that is in the lower right part of the bowl.
5. On the eighth line, write the consonant that is in the upper right part of the bowl.
6. On the fourth line, write the vowel that is in the lower left part of the bowl.
7. On the sixth line, write the vowel that is in the upper left part of the bowl.
8. On the first line, write the consonant that is in the lower left part of the bowl.

Answer: What's the word? **Ravenous!**

POTATO PUZZLE—page 10

What country did potatoes originally come from? Sometimes they are called "Irish Potatoes," but they did not come from Ireland. Follow the directions to find out.

1. Shade in all the boxes in columns A and I.
2. Now shade in the top three boxes of columns C and K.
3. Shade in all the boxes in columns M and O.
4. Shade in boxes 1, 3, and 4 of column J.
5. Shade in boxes 1, 3, and 6 of column F.
6. Also shade in boxes 1, 3, and 6 of column G.
7. Shade in the sixth box of column N.
8. Shade in all the boxes of column E.
9. Shade in boxes 1 and 3 of column B.
10. Shade in boxes 5 and 6 of column K.

Answer: Where were potatoes first grown? **Peru.**

FIX THE X-RAY—page 11

To make the x-ray work, connect these "X words" as I read them. Start with **taxi.** Ready? Let's begin.

duplex • expert • larynx • exercise • fix • coxa • exist • Texas • hex • extreme • tuxedo • extract • sixty • exact • coax • nix • exempt • tax • luxury • pox • dextrose • external • express • jinx • xylyl • axle • exquisite • ibex • ox • dexterity • exotic • xebec • Dixie • explode • ilex • six • fox • exit • exterior • axe • expose • mix • expect • wax • lox • explore • extra • oxygen • extent • next • exhaust • axiom • vex • axis • export • pixie • box • extinct.

1,840 WHATS?—page 12

In 1976, Michael Reynolds of England set a record by eating 1,840 things in 30 minutes. To find out what those things were, follow the directions.

1. In row A, circle the sixth letter.
2. In row B, circle the fourth letter.
3. In row C, circle the third letter.
4. In row D, circle the first letter.
5. In row E, circle the second letter.
6. In row F, circle the fifth letter.
7. In row G, circle the fourth letter.
8. In row H, circle the third letter.
9. In row I, circle the fourth letter.
10. In row J, circle the fifth letter.

Now read the circled letters from the **bottom up** to find out what Michael ate.

Answer: He ate 1,840 **baked beans.**

NOISY GHOST—page 13

Follow the directions to find a big word that means a noisy ghost.

1. In the first row of boxes, write **whisper.**
2. In the second row, write **spooky.**
3. In the third row, write **clank.**
4. In the fourth row, write **haunt.**
5. In the fifth row, write **creak.**
6. In the sixth row, write **mystery.**
7. In the seventh row, write **groan.**
8. In the eighth row, write **eerie.**
9. In the ninth row, write **spirit.**
10. In the tenth row, write **scream.**
11. In the eleventh row, write **phantom.**

Answer: A **poltergeist** *is a noisy ghost.*

A SKY FULL OF KITES—page 14

In 1976, a man in Japan set a record for the greatest number of kites flown from a single line. Follow the directions to find out how many kites were on that line. First, guess how many kites there were and write your guess in the box under your name. Now listen as I tell you to circle certain letters in the numbered boxes.

1. In box 1, circle the middle letter.
2. In box 2, circle the letter on the right.
3. In box 3, circle the middle letter.
4. In box 4, circle the middle letter.
5. In box 5, circle the letter on the left.
6. In box 6, do not circle any letters.
7. In box 7, circle the middle letter.
8. In box 8, circle the letter on the right.
9. In box 9, circle the letter on the right.
10. In box 10, do not circle any letters.
11. In box 11, circle the middle letter.
12. In box 12, circle the middle letter.
13. In box 13, circle the letter on the right.
14. In box 14, circle the middle letter.
15. In box 15, circle the letter on the left.
16. In box 16, circle the middle letter.
17. In box 17, circle the middle letter.
18. In box 18, circle the letter on the right.
19. In box 19, do not circle any letters.
20. In box 20, circle the letter on the right.
21. In box 21, circle the middle letter.
22. In box 22, circle the letter on the left.

Now read the circled letters **from the bottom up** to find the answer.

Answer: There were **one thousand and fifty** *kites on the line.*

TRICKY TOY—page 15

Follow the directions to spell a toy whose name comes from Greek words meaning "to see beautiful forms."

1. On the tenth line, write the letter that is in the star and the circle.
2. On the fifth line write the letter that is in the heart only.
3. On the second line write the letter that is in the heart and the circle.
4. On the eighth line write the letter that is in the star and the square.
5. On the third line write the letter that is in the half-circle only.
6. On the sixth line write the letter that is in the square only.
7. On the twelfth line write the letter that is in the half-circle and the square.
8. On the seventh line write the letter that is in the triangle only.
9. On the eleventh line write the letter that is in the circle only.
10. On the fourth line write the letter that is in the star only.
11. On the ninth line write the letter that is in the heart and the triangle.
12. On the first line write the letter that is in the triangle and the square.

Answer: The toy is a **kaleidoscope.**

FIND THE FOOD—page 16

Follow the directions to make a picture of one of the foods named below. Listen carefully!

1. Shade in pepper, but not pepperoni.
2. Shade in peas, but not pizza.
3. Shade in pumpkin and pumpernickel.
4. Shade in pork, but not poi or pie.
5. Shade in peach and pear, but not prune, pineapple, or pomegranate.
6. Do not shade in pickle or pancake.
7. Shade in popcorn and peanut.
8. Shade in pecan, but not pistachio.
9. Shade in punch, but not potato or poundcake.
10. Shade in popover, but not papaya.
11. Do not shade in paprika, but shade in peppermint.
12. Shade in pilaf and persimmon.
13. Do not shade in pastrami.
14. Shade in pudding and pretzel.

Answer: The hidden food is a **pretzel.**

WHAT HAPPENED?—page 17

What happened in this room? The police have been called to investigate the cause of this disaster. Help them solve the case by following directions.

1. If the window was left open, put a G in square 8.
2. If the guitar is on the floor, put a V in square 14.
3. If the door to the room is closed, put a P in square 2.
4. If you can see a baseball in the room, put an H in square 18.
5. If you can find a set of keys, put an S in square 16.
6. If there is food in the room, put Rs in squares 10 and 20.
7. If the piggy bank is broken, put a C in square 17.
8. If there is more than two posters on the wall, put an N in square 6.
9. If it looks as if somebody is hiding under the bed, put a T in square 3.
10. If you can find more than three shoes, put an L in square 12.
11. If there are not books on the floor, put a B in square 11.
12. If anything is hanging from the ceiling, put As in squares 1 and 7.
13. If you can find the number 17 in the room, put an I in square 13.
14. If more than two drawers are open, put Es in squares 4, 5, 9, 15, 19, and 21.

Answer: **A teenager lives here.**

HIDDEN TONGUE TWISTER—page 18

1. If honey isn't purple, put an R in circle 11.
2. If carrots don't grow on trees, put a C in circle 18.
3. If a lock is used to open a key, put an S in circle 1.
4. If a meter is longer than a centimeter, put Ls in circles 13 and 20.
5. If whales don't eat hay, put an O in circle 3.
6. If butterflies turn into caterpillars, put a G in circle 22.
7. If two times two isn't two, put an A in circle 7.
8. If snakes lose their feathers in the fall, put a W in circle 15.
9. If Halloween is in the month before November, put an I in circle 17.
10. If dinosaurs are extinct, put Ks in circles 4 and 19.
11. If jelly beans are sweeter than chili beans, put a U in circle 10.
12. If a fish can wiggle its ears, put an F in circle 6.
13. If a football isn't square, put Es in circles 5, 14, and 21.
14. If cats quack, put a B in circle 8.
15. If a goat is bigger than a goldfish, put Ps in circles 2, 9, 12, and 16.

Hidden tongue twister: **Poke a purple pickle.**

FAMOUS FOODS—page 19

Before Christopher Columbus, all of these foods had one thing in common. Follow the directions to find out what it was.

1. In the first row of boxes, write corn.
2. In the second row, write chocolate.
3. In the third row, write tomatoes.
4. In the fourth row, write pumpkins.
5. In the fifth row, write peanuts.
6. In the sixth row, write coconuts.
7. In the seventh row, write strawberries.
8. In the eighth row, write lima beans.
9. In the ninth row, write tapioca.
10. In the tenth row, write pineapples.
11. In the eleventh row, write raspberries.
12. In the twelfth row, write guavas.
13. In the thirteenth row, write red peppers.
14. In the fourteenth row, write sweet potatoes.
15. In the fifteenth row, write papayas.
16. In the sixteenth row, write potatoes.

Answer: All of these foods are native to the new world, and were **not known in Europe** *before Columbus's voyages and discoveries.*

KHAKI, CRIMSON, CHARTREUSE—
page 20

The words at the bottom of the page are names of colors. Follow the directions to match them with the descriptions of the paint tubes. Write the names of the colors in the blobs of paint coming out of the tubes. The first one is done for you.

1. The middle tube on the right holds **magenta** paint.
2. The first tube on the left holds **amber** paint.
3. The tube that is next to last on the left holds **sepia** paint.
4. The second tube on the right holds **chartreuse** paint.
5. The last tube on the left holds **vermilion** paint.
6. Tube 7 holds **khaki** paint.
7. The fifth tube on the right holds **ocher** paint.
8. The last tube on the right holds **umber** paint.
9. The third tube on the right holds **indigo** paint.
10. The first tube on the right holds **aquamarine** paint.
11. The tube that is next to last on the right holds **scarlet** paint.
12. The third tube on the left holds **crimson** paint.
13. Tube 11 holds **russet** paint.
14. The fifth tube on the left holds **maroon** paint.
15. The second tube on the left holds **azure** paint.

Answer: If you have followed the directions correctly, the color names will be in alphabetical order.

HIPPO RIDDLE—page 21

There is an old riddle that says, "Why did the chicken cross the road? To get to the other side." Now, follow directions to find out why the **hippopotamus** crossed the road. I will tell you to shade in either the vowel or the consonant in each of these boxes. In some boxes, I will tell you to shade in both letters.

1. In box 1, shade in the vowel.
2. In box 2, shade in the consonant.
3. In box 3, shade in the vowel.
4. In box 4, shade in the consonant.
5. In box 5, shade in the consonant.
6. In box 6, shade in the vowel.
7. In box 7, shade in the consonant.
8. In box 8, shade in both letters.
9. In box 9, shade in the consonant.
10. In box 10, shade in the vowel.
11. In box 11, shade in both letters.
12. In box 12, shade in the vowel.
13. In box 13, shade in the consonant.
14. In box 14, shade in the vowel.
15. In box 15, shade in both letters.
16. In box 16, shade in the vowel.
17. In box 17, shade in the consonant.
18. In box 18, shade in the consonant.
19. In box 19, shade in the vowel.
20. In box 20, shade in the vowel.
21. In box 21, shade in the consonant.
22. In box 22, shade in both letters.
23. In box 23, shade in the vowel.
24. In box 24, shade in the vowel.
25. In box 25, shade in the consonant.
26. In box 26, shade in both letters.
27. In box 27, shade in the vowel.
28. In box 28, shade in the vowel.
29. In box 29, shade in the consonant.
30. In box 30, shade in the vowel.
31. In box 31, shade in the vowel.
32. In box 32, shade in the consonant.
33. In box 33, shade in the vowel.

Answer: The hippopotamus crossed the road **because it was tied to the chicken!**

NAME THAT NOTE—page 22

The musical note on this page is known as a sixty-fourth note. It also has a longer name that's fun to say. Follow the directions to find the note's other name.

1. In the first row of squares, write **crash.**
2. In the second row, write **tweet.**
3. In the third row, write **smack.**
4. In the fourth row, write **chirp.**
5. In the fifth row, write **thud.**
6. In the sixth row, write **screech.**
7. In the seventh row, write **hum.**
8. In the eighth row, write **grind.**
9. In the ninth row, write **snap.**
10. In the tenth row, write **jingle.**
11. In the eleventh row, write **scream.**
12. In the twelfth row, write **hiss.**
13. In the thirteenth row, write **squeak.**
14. In the fourteenth row, write **slurp.**
15. In the fifteenth row, write **twang.**
16. In the sixteenth row, write **varoom.**
17. In the seventeenth row, write **rattle.**
18. In the eighteenth row, write **growl.**

Answer: The name of the note is written in the shaded rectangle. This note is a **hemidemisemiquaver.**

FIND THE FACE—page 23

Use a pencil to shade in the shapes in this puzzle. If you follow the directions correctly, you will make a picture of a face.

1. Shade in areas 4 and 6 lightly.
2. Shade in areas 2 and 21 darkly.
3. Shade in areas 20 and 43 lightly.
4. Shade in areas 40 and 41 darkly.
5. Shade in areas 11 and 17 lightly.
6. Shade in areas 13 an 31 darkly.
7. Shade in areas 8 and 38 darkly.
8. Shade in areas 1 and 37 lightly.
9. Shade in areas 33 and 39 lightly.
10. Shade in areas 3 and 35 darkly.
11. Shade in areas 5, 15, and 18 darkly.
12. Shade in areas 16 and 36 lightly.
13. Shade in areas 7 and 27 darkly.
14. Shade in area 28 lightly and area 9 darkly.
15. Shade in area 34 darkly and area 42 lightly.
16. Shade in areas 23, 30, and 32 lightly.
17. Shade in area 12 darkly and area 26 lightly.
18. Shade in area 24 darkly.

SNAKE FACTS—page 24

Follow the directions to learn some interesting facts about snakes.

1. Write the word in the first stripe on all the lines labeled X.
2. Write the word in the second stripe on the line labeled F.
3. Write the word in the third stripe on the line labeled V.
4. Write the word in the fourth stripe on the lines labeled W.
5. Write the word in the fifth stripe on the line labeled M.
6. Write the word in the sixth stripe on the line labeled R.
7. Write the word in the seventh stripe on line labeled J.
8. Write the word in the eighth stripe on the lines labeled Q.
9. Write the word in the ninth stripe on the line labeled G.
10. Write the word in the tenth stripe on the line labeled L.
11. Write the word in the eleventh stripe on line labeled P.
12. Write the word in the twelfth stripe on the line labeled C.
13. Write the word in the thirteenth stripe on the line labeled H.
14. Write the word in the fourteenth stripe on the lines labeled Z.
15. Write the word in the fifteenth stripe on the line labeled O.
16. Write the word in the sixteenth stripe on the line labeled D.
17. Write the word in the seventeenth stripe on the line labeled S.
18. Write the word in the eighteenth stripe on the line labeled B.
19. Write the word in the nineteenth stripe on the line labeled K.
20. Write the word in the twentieth stripe on the line labeled I.
21. Write the word in the twenty-first stripe on the line labeled N.
22. Write the word in the twenty-second stripe on the line labeled U.
23. Write the word in the twenty-third stripe on the line labeled A.

WHAT IS A MENAGERIE?—page 25

Follow the directions to find out what a menagerie is. In each of the four sections of this page is one animal from each of five animal groups: mammal, bird, fish, reptile, and insect.

1. In the first square, write the first letter of the **insect** in the **upper right** section of the page.
2. In the second square, write the first letter of the **bird** in the **upper left** section.
3. In the third square, write the first letter of the **mammal** in the **lower left** section.
4. In the fourth square, write the first letter of the **insect** in the **lower left** section.
5. In the fifth square, write the first letter of the **bird** in the **lower left** section.
6. In the sixth square, write the first letter of the **fish** in the **upper left** section.
7. In the seventh square, write the first letter of the **reptile** in the **lower left** section.
8. In the eighth square, write the first letter of the **reptile** in the **upper right** section.
9. In the ninth square, write the first letter of the **mammal** in the **lower right** section.
10. In the tenth square, write the first letter of the **mammal** in the **upper left** section.
11. In the eleventh square, write the first letter of the **bird** in the **lower right** section.
12. In the twelfth square, write the first letter of the **bird** in the **upper right** section.
13. In the thirteenth square, write the first letter of the **insect** in the **lower right** section.
14. In the fourteenth square, write the first letter of the **reptile** in the **lower right** section.
15. In the fifteenth square, write the first letter of the **fish** in the **lower right** section.
16. In the sixteenth square, write the first letter of the **reptile** in the **upper left** section.
17. In the seventeenth square, write the first letter of the **insect** in the **upper left** section.
18. In the eighteenth square, write the first letter of the **fish** in the **lower left** section.
19. In the nineteenth square, write the first letter of the **mammal** in the **upper right** section.
20. In the twentieth square, write the first letter of the **fish** in the **upper right** section.

Answer: A menagerie is a **collection of animals.**

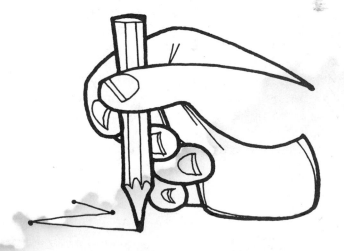